FIGHTING FAIR FOR FAMILIES

Fran Schmidt
Alice Friedman
Drawings by Rebecca Poole-Heyne
Cover illustration by Noelle Bowles

P.O. Box 191153, Miami Beach, Florida 33119

ISBN 1-878227-04-1

ACKNOWLEDGEMENTS

For their helpful ideas, we thank Glenn Schmidt, Lori Packlick, Irene Moreda, Kathy Morrow, Carol Bregman, Laura Schmidt, Ralph Schmidt and Warren Hoskins.
A special thanks to Chris Heyne.

FOREWORD

We all want to be good parents. But there are times... when parenting is difficult and exhausting. We want to escape from the people we dearly love. We wonder why life isn't more simple and why everyone can't get along just like the families on television.

Then there are times when we find ourselves impatient and irritable. Our anger turns us into Jekyll and Hyde. We let little hassles get the best of us.

Please don't get discouraged. ***FIGHTING FAIR FOR FAMILIES*** offers you the tools to handle conflict like a 'pro.' Think of yourself as a Michelangelo or a Picasso with the power to create a more loving and caring environment for you and your family.

Take the time to read and discuss this book with your family BEFORE you are emotionally involved in a conflict. Put your FIGHTING FAIR poster on the refrigerator or some other prominent spot and make it a meaningful part of your life. Good luck!

Is Your Home a Battlefield?

Does anger take over and reason go out the window?

You are not alone.

Conflict Is OK!

Conflict is a natural part of life. It is not conflict that tears families apart but the way in which conflict is handled.

We are not all the same. Each family member is unique. We see and value things differently. We have different expectations. As a result of these differences, conflicts occur.

Violence Is <u>Not</u> OK!

We can't avoid conflicts, but we can learn to "fight fair." Fighting Fair means attacking the problem, and not the person.

- Name Calling
- Blaming
- Sneering
- Not Listening
- Getting Even
- Bringing up the past
- Threats
- Pushing
- Hitting
- Put-Downs
- Bossing
- Making Excuses
- Not Taking Responsibility

FOULS are weapons which attack people, not problems. These weapons damage and destroy relationships. **FOULS** cause conflict to escalate.

Recognize **FOULS**. Work together, as a family, to eliminate them.

Fouls Don't Work

"DON'T BLAME ME,
I DIDN'T DO IT."
"MAKE ME."

"YOU BETTER CLEAN UP THIS MESS
YOUR DOG MADE."
"YOU'RE NOT PERFECT YOURSELF."

"YOU NEVER DO ANYTHING RIGHT, STUPID."
"IT'S ALL YOUR FAULT!"

Fouls attack the dignity of the people we love. They cause feelings of resentment, hatred, revenge, and destroy family relationships.

Fouls are bad habits. You have within you the power to change these destructive habits. Learn to fight fair.

Rules For Fighting Fair

We learn rules for driving, for sports, and games, but most of us have never learned rules for dealing with conflict. The Rules for Fighting Fair help families deal with conflict constructively within a caring and loving framework.

1. Identify the problem.
2. Focus on the problem.
3. Attack the ***problem***, not the person.
4. ***Listen*** with an ***open mind***.
5. Treat a person's feelings with respect.
6. Take responsibility for your actions.

Fighting Fair Works

Fighting Fair:

- ★ attacks problems not people
- ★ helps everyone involved to find solutions
- ★ protects everyone's dignity
- ★ heals hurt feelings
- ★ gives people control over their lives
- ★ builds relationships based on truth and trust
- ★ helps people take responsibility for their behavior
- ★ keeps the doors of communication open

When Anger Flares...

**When anger and tempers flare,
we cannot think or communicate clearly.
We say and do things
which cause conflict to escalate.
We forget to fight fair.**

When you are really angry, don't take it out on the ones you love. GIVE YOURSELF (and others) TIME TO COOL DOWN.

It's OK to say, "I am angry and I need time to cool down. We'll talk later."

Trust your family to understand how you feel.

Cool Down!

Call a friend.
Soak in the tub.
Scrub a floor.
Scream in your pillow.

Take a walk.
Bake a cake.
Listen to music.
Mow the lawn.

Encourage every family member to find acceptable ways to cool down. Anger is normal. Everyone has feelings. When feelings are respected, understood and cared about, trust and love grow.

There's A Time...

Bad timing can actually start a conflict.

And A Place

"Is this a good time to talk?"

"Let's discuss this over coffee after dinner."

"I'm glad that you didn't bring this up in front of my friends."

Be careful to choose an appropriate time and place for discussing touchy subjects. Be sensitive to each other's feelings. The last people we want to hurt are our family members.

"You...!"

YOU NEVER...

YOU SHOULD HAVE...

YOU MADE ME...

"You" messages are fouls and escalate conflicts. "You" messages tend to blame, label, judge, boss, or threaten. These messages cause our loved ones to become defensive.

Learning to communicate in a caring way is essential to a healthy family relationship.

Use Caring Language

Mom, I feel angry when you open my mail. Please respect my privacy.
I apologize.

1. Use the person's name.*
2. Tell how you feel.
3. Identify the problem.
4. Tell what you want done.

*When individuals are called by their names, it gets their attention, acknowledges them as a person, and opens communication.

Caring communication begins with non-blaming language, helps both sides listen to and understand each other, and gives a non-threatening message about how you perceive the problem. Caring language lets the people you love know that they are important and respected.

Learn to say "I apologize." This kind of admission of responsibility has the power to de-fuse a conflict situation and gets the conflict under control.

LISTEN...

It's difficult to listen when your feelings are hurt. Remember when you're hurting, your loved ones are hurting, too. Listening is essential to understanding the problem and to healing the hurt. None of us want to talk or listen to another person if we feel we are not respected.

Too often in a conflict, we tend to look at our side only. Listening with an open mind means listening to the other side... really listening.

With An Open Mind

Fine-tune your listening skills and discover new things about your loved ones and yourself.

- ★ Take time to listen. Try not to interrupt or think ahead to your response.
- ★ Check to make sure you understand. Say in your own words what you think the other person said. Be sure not to put words in someone else's mouth.
- ★ Watch body language, yours and theirs. Body language may be telling more than what the person can say in words.
- ★ Focus on feelings without judging them good or bad. *"How did that make you feel?" "You seem angry. Want to talk?"*
- ★ Use a non-threatening tone of voice.
- ★ Use encouraging phrases which communicate how much you care. *"Tell me about it." "Then what happened?"*
- ★ Give nonverbal encouragement — a smile, a hug, a nod, a touch.
- ★ Ask questions when something is not clear. Avoid "why" questions, which tend to blame and put people on the defensive. *"I'm not sure I understand. What happened first?"*
- ★ Allow for disagreement. Permitting your loved ones to disagree with you shows that you can listen with an open mind.

Identify the Problem

WHAT IS REALLY BOTHERING ME?

WHAT IS UPSETTING HER?

WHAT DO WE BOTH WANT?

Think of conflict as a common problem to be solved, so that solutions can be found for the mutual benefit of the whole family.

Each one involved in the conflict should state the problem from his/her own point of view.

Separate issues from personality.

Keep the conflict manageable. Bringing in too many issues at one time makes it more difficult to find workable solutions.

Change from "You ought to..." to "What can we do?"

Focus on the Problem

AVOID TRAPS

Fouls are traps and don't solve problems. If the other person uses a foul, don't fall into the trap.

Dealing with the immediate conflict will take all your energy. Don't divert your energy from the problem to be solved. Stick to the problem, and remember the rules for fighting fair.

Brainstorm for Solutions

?
Let's see how many ways we can solve the conflict.

Conflict can open up a world of possibilities when people's energy is used to attack problems and not each other. Brainstorm for creative solutions. Let your imagination go! One idea will generate more ideas. Don't reject any idea no matter how crazy it might sound.

Let everyone involved in the conflict work together for solutions.

Avoid a preconceived solution.

Lighten Up!

★ **No one is perfect.**

★ **Find humor in a situation.**

★ **Every conflict is not a tragedy.**

★ **Don't make a mountain out of a molehill.**

★ **Don't be afraid to laugh at yourself.**

Be a Mediator

There are times when family members cannot solve their problems on their own. They need the help of a mediator.

A mediator listens to both sides and helps the people in a conflict come to a fair agreement.

The goal of mediation is to solve a problem, not to blame or punish.

Here's How

Set the ground rules:

★Listen without interrupting.
★Be willing to solve the problem.
★Tell the truth.
★No fouls.

Each side tells his/her story.

Each side tells how he/she feels.

Both think of several solutions to the problem.

Both pick the solution they think they can live with.

Each side is responsible for carrying out the agreed upon solution.

Everyone in the family can learn to be a mediator.

Home Sweet...

A Fighting Fair family still fights, still has problems, still has frustrations, but now has a framework to resolve these conflicts, keeping everyone's dignity intact.

Let family members know you love them and care about them.

- ★ **Talk with your children**
- ★ **Talk about feelings**
- ★ **Do things together**
- ★ **Work together**
- ★ **Help each other**
- ★ **Hug each other**

Sanctuary

Fighting Fair changes a family battlefield into a sanctuary – a sanctuary where "wounds" are healed, mistakes forgiven, feelings listened to, and fear replaced with trust and security — a place that nurtures each precious member of your family. Relax and enjoy the uniqueness that each of you contributes to the family.

Best wishes!

A peaceful world begins with a peaceful family.

Would you like your child to learn more about handling conflict constructively?

The Peace Education Foundation also publishes educational materials which teach students to deal creatively and constructively with conflict. Please send us your child's school's name, address, and principal's name. We will send them our brochure describing the curricula.

- ▲ Peacemaking Skills for Little Kids (Preschool-2)
- ▲ Creative Conflict Solving for Kids: Grades 3-4
- ▲ Creative Conflict Solving for Kids: Grades 5-9
- ▲ Mediation for Kids (Grades 4-9)
- ▲ Fighting Fair: Dr. Martin Luther King, Jr. for Kids (Grades 4-9)
- ▲ Come In Spaceship Earth: Kids as Crew Members (Grades 4-9)
- ▲ Young Voices: Student Essays on Peace

The Peace Education Foundation also offers workshops on Conflict Resolution, Mediation, and Peacemaking.

For information write:
Peace Education Foundation
P.O. Box 191153, Miami Beach, FL 33119

I would like my child to learn more about conflict management at school.

My students just love Conflict Solving for Kids. *They enjoy all of the activities and I can honestly say that the program has made a significant difference in the way the children treat each other. Name calling and put downs are rarely heard and when they occur they are handled before they turn into a fight.*

Joanne Sweeney
Fifth Grade Teacher,
New York

School Referral Form

My name is:

Name ______________________

Address ______________________

____

City ______________________

State ______________ Zip ________

Phone (______)______________________

My child's name is:

____

____

Grade ______________________

My child's school is:

School ______________________

Address ______________________

____

City ______________________

State ______________ Zip ________

Phone (______)______________________

Principal's name is:

____

Teacher's name is:

____

"Invaluable. A must for every classroom."
Joan Watson, Parkway Elementary

School Referral Form

My name is:

Name ______________________

Address ______________________

____

City ______________________

State ______________ Zip ________

Phone (______)______________________

My child's name is:

____

____

Grade ______________________

My child's school is:

School ______________________

Address ______________________

____

City ______________________

State ______________ Zip ________

Phone (______)______________________

Principal's name is:

____

Teacher's name is:

____

AFFIX
STAMP
HERE

FOUNDATION, INC.

P.O. Box 191153
Miami Beach, FL 33119

Please Feel Free to Use an Envelope.

AFFIX
STAMP
HERE

FOUNDATION, INC.

P.O. Box 191153
Miami Beach, FL 33119

Order Form

Fighting Fair For Families		QTY.	TOTAL
FM Illustrated Book and Poster (Price includes $2.00 for insured shipping and handling)	$11.95	☐	$ ______
Brochure of School Curricula and Workshops for Professionals in Education and Youth Development	N/C	☐	
Florida customers add 6% sales tax. **Dade County** add 6.5% sales tax. **Canadian Orders** add 7% G.S.T. or give exemption number			$ ______
Outside U.S. add $2.00 additional shipping per unit			$ ______
Tax Exempt I.D. No. ______	TOTAL (U.S. Dollars)		$ ______

Name ______ Title ______

School or Organization ______

Billing Address ______ **Shipping Address** ______

______ Customs Broker ______

City/State/Zip ______ City/State/Zip ______

Phone (___) ______ Ext ______ Phone (___) ______ Ext ______

Make checks payable to:

Peace Education Foundation, Inc.
2627 Biscayne Boulevard
Miami, Florida 33137-3854
TELEPHONE INQUIRIES (305) 576-5075

I choose to use my credit card.

(Circle One)

VISA MasterCard

"We Welcome"

Expiration Date Required

MasterCard Inter Bank No. (Above Your Name)

Signature ______

24-HOUR FAX ORDER LINE (305) 576-3106
Order at your convenience. Public and Parochial Schools may place orders by telefax. Complete this Order Form and **FAX-IT** with accompanying purchase order to speed delivery.

PAYMENT MUST ACCOMPANY ORDERS FROM INDIVIDUALS AND PRIVATE ORGANIZATIONS. Payment is due 30 days after receipt of materials on orders from public and parochial institutions. School and institutional purchase orders must be signed and approved by personnel authorized to place orders and/or make payment. **U.S. FUNDS ONLY. NO TELEPHONE ORDERS PLEASE.**

Order Form

Fighting Fair For Families		QTY.	TOTAL
FM Illustrated Book and Poster (Price includes $2.00 for insured shipping and handling)	$11.95	☐	$ ______
Brochure of School Curricula and Workshops for Professionals in Education and Youth Development	N/C	☐	
Florida customers add 6% sales tax. **Dade County** add 6.5% sales tax. **Canadian Orders** add 7% G.S.T. or give exemption number			$ ______
Outside U.S. add $2.00 additional shipping per unit			$ ______
Tax Exempt I.D. No. ______	TOTAL (U.S. Dollars)		$ ______

Name ______ Title ______

School or Organization ______

Billing Address ______ **Shipping Address** ______

______ Customs Broker ______

City/State/Zip ______ City/State/Zip ______

Phone (___) ______ Ext ______ Phone (___) ______ Ext ______

Make checks payable to:

Peace Education Foundation, Inc.
2627 Biscayne Boulevard
Miami, Florida 33137-3854
TELEPHONE INQUIRIES (305) 576-5075

I choose to use my credit card.

(Circle One)

VISA MasterCard

"We Welcome"

Expiration Date Required

MasterCard Inter Bank No. (Above Your Name)

Signature ______

24-HOUR FAX ORDER LINE (305) 576-3106
Order at your convenience. Public and Parochial Schools may place orders by telefax. Complete this Order Form and **FAX-IT** with accompanying purchase order to speed delivery.

PAYMENT MUST ACCOMPANY ORDERS FROM INDIVIDUALS AND PRIVATE ORGANIZATIONS. Payment is due 30 days after receipt of materials on orders from public and parochial institutions. School and institutional purchase orders must be signed and approved by personnel authorized to place orders and/or make payment. **U.S. FUNDS ONLY. NO TELEPHONE ORDERS PLEASE.**

Let us ship your Fighting Fair for Families gift order direct.

Gift is for:

Name ______________________________

Address ______________________________

City ____________________ State __________ Zip __________

Other family member's names:

____

____

A lovely gift card will accompany your Fighting Fair for Families Gift order which says:

With all best wishes

Signed:

____

____

____

A Great Gift for Friends!

Let us ship your Fighting Fair for Families gift order direct.

Gift is for:

Name ______________________________

Address ______________________________

City ____________________ State __________ Zip __________

Other family member's names:

____

____

A lovely gift card will accompany your Fighting Fair for Families Gift order which says:

With all best wishes

Signed:

____

____

____